First Facts®

Expert Pet Care

CARING for Rabbits

by Tammy Gagne

Consultant:
Jennifer Zablotny, DVM
Member, American Veterinary Medical Association

PEBBLE
a capstone imprint

First Facts are published by Pebble
1710 Roe Crest Drive, North Mankato, Minnesota 56003
capstonepub.com

Library of Congress Cataloging-in-Publication Data
is available on the Library of Congress website.

ISBN 978-1-5435-2743-8 (library binding)
ISBN 978-1-5435-2749-0 (paperback)
ISBN 978-1-5435-2755-1 (ebook pdf)

Editorial Credits
Marissa Kirkman, editor; Sarah Bennett, designer; Tracy Cummins, media researcher; Laura Manthe, production specialist

Photo Credits
Alamy: Rosanne Tackaberry, 16; Capstone Studio: Karon Dubke, 7, 13, 19; Getty Images: Rebecca Emery, 17; iStockphoto: bunnylovinggrl, 6, cnicbc, 12, kali9, 15; Shutterstock: Africa Studio, 11 Bottom, Casey Williamson, 5, Dorottya Mathe, 21 Middle, Ear Iew Boo, 8, ekmelica, Design Element, Eric Isselee, 21 Bottom Left, IrinaK, 21 Bottom Right, JIANG HONGYAN, 3, Julia Kuznetsova, 9, kai_foret, 10, Linn Currie, 21 Top Right, Oleksandr Lytvynenko, Back Cover, 24, Olhastock, Cover, 23, Pentium5, 20, Santhosh Varghese, 11 Top, soportography, 18.

Printed in the United States   5844

Table of Contents

Your New Pet Rabbit

Rabbits are smart and playful pets. They are quiet pets that do not need much space. It is fun to watch them hop around. A rabbit may be the perfect pet for you. Make sure you are ready for this **responsibility** before getting a pet.

There are many different kinds of rabbits. Your family will need to choose which type of rabbit to bring home.

Look for a rabbit at a **shelter**. Many homeless animals can be found there.

responsibility—a duty or a job

 shelter—a place that takes care of lost or stray animals

Supplies You Will Need

You will need to buy supplies for your rabbit, including a **hutch** or a cage. This is where your pet will sleep and spend time. Make sure the hutch is big enough for your pet to hop around. Your rabbit will also need bedding for its cage, such as straw.

Your rabbit will need bowls for food and water. You can also use a water bottle for your pet. Be sure to buy chew toys for your rabbit too.

Some rabbit owners train their pets to use litter boxes. These rabbits often spend more time outside their cages.

 hutch—a cage used to hold rabbits or other small pets

OXBOW
ANIMAL HEALTH
ORCHARD GRASS HAY
Hand selected
KAYTEE
Fiesta max

Bringing Your Rabbit Home

Bringing your rabbit home is exciting. Many pet rabbits live in homes with cats and dogs. But be careful around other pets. A large dog could hurt a rabbit.

The best companion for a pet rabbit is another rabbit. Many owners say that it is easier to care for two rabbits than one. Rabbits are often more happy and friendly when kept together.

Guinea pigs also make good companions for rabbits.

What Do Rabbits Eat?

Feed your rabbit hay each day. You can also give it a small amount of **pellets**. They contain many **vitamins** your pet needs to stay healthy. Your rabbit will also need fresh water. Be sure to fill the bowl or bottle each day.

You can also feed small amounts of leafy green vegetables. Most rabbits eat parsley and spinach. Rabbits also eat carrots and the green tops on them.

Never give your rabbit corn, iceberg lettuce, potatoes, or rhubarb. These foods can make your pet sick.

pellet—a small, hard piece of food; pellets give animals the nutrition they need

vitamin—a nutrient that helps keep people and animals healthy

This rabbit is eating pellets.

Cleaning Time

Rabbits stay clean by licking themselves. But you must also brush your pet. This helps your pet **shed** fur less often. It also keeps your rabbit from swallowing loose fur when cleaning itself.

Change your rabbit's straw bedding each day. You will also need to clean the cage about once a week. Staying clean and dry will help keep your pet healthy.

If you place a small bin at one end of the cage, your pet will likely use it as a bathroom. This will make cleaning the cage a lot easier.

 shed—to lose hair

Going to the Vet

Rabbits need to visit a **veterinarian** just like other pets. Take your rabbit once a year for a checkup. You will also need to take your rabbit to a vet if it gets sick.

It is smart to have your rabbit **spayed** or **neutered**. This keeps rabbits from having babies. It also makes your rabbit a calmer and healthier pet.

Rabbits can be spayed or neutered once they are six months old.

veterinarian—a doctor trained to take care of animals

spay—to operate on a female animal so it is unable to produce young

neuter—to operate on a male animal so it is unable to produce young

Life with a Rabbit

Regular exercise keeps rabbits healthy. Make sure to take your rabbit out of its cage for a few hours each day.

Some people keep their rabbit hutches outside. But it is good for rabbits to be near people too. The best places for a rabbit cage are often a living room or family room.

Rabbits chew everything in sight. It is important to watch your pet when it is outside its cage.

Your Rabbit Through the Years

Rabbits are full of energy. Even adult rabbits spend a good deal of time hopping and playing. But as your rabbit gets older, some changes will take place.

Rabbits who are five years or older are called **senior** pets. Your older rabbit will rest more and play less than it did before. Senior rabbits can become overweight if owners are not careful. You may need to cut back on the amount of pellets you feed your senior pet.

senior—older than someone else; a senior pet is an older animal

When well cared for, rabbits can live
between eight and 12 years.

Rabbit Body Language

You can watch your rabbit's **behavior** to know how it is feeling. An excited rabbit will run and jump in a dancing motion. This move is called a binky. A rabbit that feels safe will quickly roll onto its side. This is called a flop.

An angry rabbit will sometimes growl. It is important to leave your rabbit alone if it makes this sound.

  behavior—the way a person or an animal acts

Types of Rabbits

Longhaired rabbits:
- Angora rabbits
- Jersey wooly rabbits
- Lionhead rabbits

Jersey wooly rabbit

Lionhead rabbit

Belgian hare

Shorthaired rabbits:
- American rabbits
- Belgian hares
- Dutch rabbits

Dutch rabbit

Glossary

behavior (bee-HAY-vyuhr)—the way a person or an animal acts

hutch (HUHCH)—a cage used to hold rabbits or other small pets

neuter (NOO-tur)—to operate on a male animal so it is unable to produce young

pellet (PEL-it)—a small, hard piece of food; pellets give animals the nutrition they need

responsibility (ri-spon-suh-BIL-uh-tee)—a duty or a job

senior (SEE-nyur)—older than someone else; a senior pet is an older animal

shed (SHED)—to lose hair

shelter (SHEL-tur)—a place that takes care of lost or stray animals

spay (SPAY)—to operate on a female animal so it is unable to produce young

veterinarian (vet-ur-uh-NER-ee-uhn)—a doctor trained to take care of animals

vitamin (VYE-tuh-min)—a nutrient that helps keep people and animals healthy

Read More

Ganeri, Anita. *Bunny's Guide to Caring for Your Rabbit*. Pets' Guides. Chicago: Capstone Heinemann Library, 2013.

Gardeski, Christina Mia. *Pet Rabbits: Questions and Answers*. Pet Questions and Answers. North Mankato, Minn.: Capstone Press, 2017.

Murray, Julie. *Rabbits*. Everyday Animals. Minneapolis: ABDO Kids, 2016.

Critical Thinking Questions

1. Why is it important to watch your rabbit closely while it is out of its cage?

2. What foods are dangerous for your pet rabbit?

3. How can you tell if your rabbit is excited?

Index